"Do You Hear Me?"

Laughs
for the Hard of Hearing
by the Hard of Hearing

Maxwell Schneider

Thinking Publications
Eau Claire, Wisconsin

Library of Congress Cataloging-in-Publication Data

Schneider, Maxwell
    "Do you hear me?" : laughs for the hard of hearing by the hard of hear-
ing / by Maxwell Schneider.
        p.   cm.
    ISBN 0-930599-45-4 (pbk.)
    1. Hearing impaired—Humor.   I. Title.
PN6231.D333S36   1996
818'.5402—dc20
                                              96-35158
                                              CIP

Clown illustrations by Patti Argoff

**THINKING
PUBLICATIONS**®
A Division of McKinley Companies, Inc.

424 Galloway Street • Eau Claire, WI 54703
(800) 225-GROW • FAX (800) 828-8885
E-mail: custserv@ThinkingPublications.com • www.ThinkingPublications.com

*This book is dedicated to the more than
24 million Americans
who are hard of hearing and whose
"pursuit of happiness"
is made that much more difficult
because of their disability.*

Acknowledgments

It is truly impossible to list the names of all those who helped make *"Do You Hear Me?"* a reality. Everyone, it seems, wanted to help, because everyone knows the undeniably wonderful therapy of humor. There are some, however, whose efforts were so heroic that they must be mentioned here. I name just a few: Bill Paschell of the Washington Area Group for the Hard of Hearing (WAGHOH); Dr. Sidney Busis, Pittsburgh, PA; Dr. Charles Diggs of the American Speech-Language-Hearing Association (ASHA); J.J. Rizzo, Executive Director of the Better Hearing Institute; and the library staffs of Boca Raton and Delray Beach, FL.

And to all my friends and family, my heartfelt thanks. Your words of encouragement were so very sincere that, believe it or not, they continued to come through loud and clear even after the batteries in my hearing aid had expired!

Introduction

Hearing impairment has various causes, but it was gunfire during basic training in World War II that cost me much of my own. Hearing aids are a wonderful assist, but occasionally I'll have a problem typical of those with less than normal hearing. It didn't take me long to recognize that, under such circumstances, *a sense of humor can be a lifesaver,* and I lean on mine as one does on a cane.

"Do You Hear Me?"—the *little* book with a *big* mission—is a collection of all those things that helped me cope with my hearing problems, cartoons that made me laugh,

jokes that brought chuckles even though I might have had to ask for a repeat or two of the punchline, and stories of "mix-ups" sent to me from everywhere when word got around that I was looking for a way to relieve the tensions and frustrations of those who are hard of hearing (HOH).

All these, plus my own experiences, are presented in the hopes they will do for you what they did for me. Start smiling and all those potholes on the road we travel will begin to disappear, for believe you me, humor can indeed be one of life's greatest shock absorbers.

Maxwell Schneider

SO
WHAT CAN BE
AMUSING ABOUT BEING
HARD OF HEARING?

THIS!

THIS is what can be
amusing when the hearing is
somewhat less than
"20/20."

*"I **distinctly** said bandannas!"*

AND THIS!

From this point on, you're
on your own!

➤ I thought my wife, Barbara, was losing her hearing, so one day I decided to test it. I quietly walked in the front door and stood 30 feet behind her.

"Barbara," I said, "can you hear me?" There was no response, so I moved to 20 feet behind her.

"Barbara," I repeated, "can you hear me?" Still no reply. I advanced to 10 feet and asked, "Now can you hear me?"

"Yes dear," Barbara answered. "For the *third* time, *yes!*"

D.O.H. in Reader's Digest

➤ Two friends meet and exchange greetings. Then Bob, who is HOH, says to John, "My whole life has changed. I'm wearing a new hearing aid that's a marvel of the latest developments in electronic ingenuity. It cost me $6,000, but it's worth every penny. It's absolutely the greatest!"

John says, "That's wonderful. What kind is it?" Bob looks at his watch and says, "It's a quarter past four."

➤ I never knew that hearing impairment can come and go, but twice now when I've asked my boss for a raise, he's been afflicted.

➤ A speaker on a platform, addressing a group of people without benefit of a microphone, raises his voice and says, "Can you people in back hear me?" A man up front says, "What?"

Positive Aspects of Being HOH:

➤ You find you honestly don't hear what you used to pretend you didn't hear.

➤ Your friends will trust you with a secret. What they don't know is that you probably didn't hear it in the first place.

➤ People appreciate the fact that they don't have to talk about you behind your back; as long as they keep smiling, they can talk about you in front of your face.

The ultimate hearing aid for talking to yourself.

11

A Little Story

➤ A fellow calls his friend long distance and asks him to lend him $10,000.

His friend says, "Eh? What did you say? Huh? What? Who? Er, what? WHAT??"

The fellow repeats, "I need $10,000. I want you to lend me $10,000."

Friend: "Huh? What'd ya say? Who? What? What'zat?"

The fellow: *"Lend me $10,000! $10,000!"*

Friend: "What? I don't catch it. What? Say it again. Who?"

Whereupon the operator cuts in and says, "He's trying to tell you he wants you to lend him $10,000."

The friend says to the operator, *"**You** heard him. **You** give it to him!"*

Hearing is with the ears; *listening* is with the mind and heart:

Two men were fishing one day. The partner who was hard of hearing hooked a beautiful five-pound bass. The fish put up a courageous battle, and it was 20 minutes before the fisherman boated him.

While his fishing partner looked on in disbelief and hollered and yelled in protest, he gently unhooked and released the fish.

"I wanted that fish," his distraught partner shouted. "Didn't you hear me?"

"Oh, I heard *you* alright, but it was the *fish* I was listening to."

*You have **so** got it turned off!*

A Little Story

 A woman who is hard of hearing visits her doctor. "I don't know exactly what's bothering me," she says, "but I'm feeling low, and even my hearing seems to have gotten worse."

The doctor examines her eyes and finds nothing to be concerned about there. Next he looks into her throat and that's OK. He looks into her right ear and that's fine;

then he peers into her left ear. At this point, he removes his glasses, cleans them, and looks again. He reaches into his cabinet for a pair of forceps, and with them removes something from the ear.

Shaking his head slowly, he says, "It's hard to believe, but this looks like a suppository."

"Oh!" she says, "Thank you! Thank you!! Now I know where I put my hearing aid."

"Do You Hear Me?"
Revises *Webster's Dictioneary*

Webster's	Our Spelling	Our *Deaf*inition
hereafter	h*ear*after	To "get it" later.
hereby	h*ear*by	Whatever helps your hearing.
heretofore	h*eart*ofore	What you thought you heard before.

*Deaf*initions—Continued

Webster's	Our Spelling	Our *Deaf*inition
herewith	h*ear*with	See hereby.
here's to you	h*ear*'s to you	Favorite toast of the HOH.
here and gone	h*ear* and gone	Was offended and left.

I like to go dancing,
Tho I can't hear the beat.
But I pick up the vibes
Thru the soles of my feet.
That system ain't bad,
But it still has its faults;
I once danced the tango
When the band played a waltz.

L. Margolis, Uniontown, PA

*"...and now notice the difference with the hearing aid **in**..."*

A Little Story

➤ Charlie was HOH, and his supervisor at work constantly made fun of him because of it. The teasing bothered Charlie so much that he decided to get another job.

He took correspondence courses and moonlighted on other jobs to get the training and experience he felt he needed to get into another field.

Finally, the day came when he was able to qualify for another job, and it was with great satisfaction that he told his supervisor he was leaving for better employment.

"Hey Charlie, I'd like to get a job like that too. How did you arrange it?" the supervisor asked.

"I upped *my* qualifications," Charlie said. "Up *yours.*"

➤ In self-defense, I'm going to have to get a more powerful hearing aid. My wife has taken to getting my attention by digging her nails into my arm or throwing things at me.

I'm both lacerated and contused, as well as HOH and confused.

Don Roda, Pennsylvania

"Do You Hear Me?"

Drawing by Ton Smits; © 1956, 1984 by *The New Yorker* Magazine, Inc. Reprinted with permission.

25

➤ A woman who was HOH ordered a Danish pastry at a coffee counter. "Would you like me to heat it for you?" the attendant politely asked. He was startled by the glare the customer gave him as she backed away and said, "What makes you think I'm not capable of eating it myself?"

➤ Rock music performances could very well advertise that their programs offer an opportunity for "Free Ear Piercing."

➤ Atlantic City is considering a beauty contest for "lovelies" who are HOH. The winner is to be crowned "Miss Understood."

A Little Story

➤ My wife felt that it would improve my hearing if I took a lip-reading course. I thought I was doing pretty well with my hearing aid but decided to please her, so I signed up for the lessons that were being offered at our local college.

Because the teacher was young and attractive and the lessons proved helpful, I repeated the course a second time and was considering repeating it a third time when my wife decided to attend one session to find out why I appeared to be having problems with the course.

She took one look at the teacher, and that was the end of my lip-reading lessons. My wife pronounced me graduated, and we went home so she could celebrate.

The lessons did help, and there was one interesting aftermath. My teacher had worn a deep crimson lipstick that made her lips a real pleasure to read, and to this day, when I see a woman wearing that particular shade of lipstick, I will immediately strike up a conversation with her.

B. Abravenel, Boca Raton, FL

➤ **It's really not so bad being HOH when...**

- A 300-pound bully insults your wife at a bar.

- Your home is under the main flight path to a major airport.

- The teenager next door digs hard rock with 18-inch speakers.

- Your wife suggests mowing the lawn, washing the car, cleaning the garage...

- Your wife says she has a bad headache.

Life After Death

When as I die from age or ill,
   And there I lie, stone cold and still,
When as you stare around my shroud,
   Good friends, beware, don't talk too loud...
For though my soul's
   No longer perking,
My hearing aid
   May still be working!

The Hearing Aid Journal
Mrs. S. Pendergrass, South Carolina

➤ My answering machine has adjusted itself to my hearing problem. After you leave a message, it says, "Would you mind repeating that?"

➤ If you want to find out what it means to "make a mountain out of a molehill," try telling a joke to a person who is HOH.

More Excerpts from the
"Do You Hear Me?" Dictione*ary*

Webster's	Our Spelling	Our *Deaf*inition
hero	h*earo*	Male lead, "Children of a Lesser God."
heroine	h*earo*ine	Female lead, same play.
heroics	h*earo*ics	The effort the HOH make to hear.

*Deaf*initions—Continued

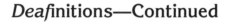

Webster's	**Our Spelling**	**Our *Deaf*inition**
Hirohito	Hearohito	WW2 emperor who turned a deaf ear to his wiser advisors.
Hereford	Hearford	Breed of steer with keen hearing.
Hercules	Hearcules	Deity of the HOH.

A Little Story

➤ A gas station owner had needed a hearing aid for much too long, but he kept putting it off. One day he was standing in his station when an attractive woman in a convertible drove in. He made it a point to take care of her before his employee could.

After he filled her tank, cleaned her windshield, and checked her oil, he thought she asked if he had a whisk broom. "No," he replied, "but I do have a vacuum cleaner; we can clean you out with that."

The woman got a furious look on her face and zoomed out the driveway. The owner, looking around in confusion, saw his employee rolling on the ground laughing. "Oh man!" the employee howled, "I don't know what you thought she said, but she asked for a *restroom!*"

Shirley Albright, California

➤ I once tried to define the word *acoustic* to a man who was HOH, and he told me that he thought it was something you used when shooting pool.

➤ Is it true that the Walkman gizmos that go on the ears are called "hear muffs"?

"Do You Hear Me?"

"I said there isn't much point in your ordering a sizzling platter if your hearing aid is out of order."

A Little (True) Story

➤ The owner of a men's clothing store ran a very successful operation. He was a real sharpie. He outfitted each of his salespeople with a fake, easy-to-see hearing aid.

When a customer asked the price of a piece of clothing, the salesperson would look for a price tag, and not finding one, would yell back to the owner, "Hey Mr. Barnes, what's the price of this garment?"

Mr. Barnes would shout back, "Sixty dollars."

The salesperson, pretending to have misunderstood him, would say, "Fifty dollars."

The result was almost always a sale.

Often, the customer would try to buy something additional, hoping for a repeat performance.

A Little Story

➤ Two friends, George and Clyde, businessmen from England, are winding up a summerlong visit to the United States. Clyde is HOH. They are sitting at a bar in New York City, and George strikes up a conversation with a man sitting next to him.

The man, recognizing the English accent, tells George he has just returned from a visit to London.

"What'd'e say?" asks Clyde in a whisper.

"'e says 'e's just come back from London," replied George. Turning to the man, George asks him what he'd enjoyed most about the city.

The man says that he particularly liked Picadilly Circus, and that he had supped at the famous Hare and Hound Pub, which he thought was outstanding.

Clyde whispers to George again, "What'd'e say?"

"'e says 'e's been to Picadilly and, fancy this, 'e visited our favorite pub, the Hare and Hound," George replies.

"And while I was at the bar," the man continues, "I was approached by a slim, good-looking, red-haired woman who invited me to visit with her at her flat just around the corner from the pub. Seems her husband was away on vacation. Boy oh boy, what a visit that was!"

Clyde tugs at George's sleeve and says, "What'd'e say?" George turns to Clyde, pauses a long moment, and then says, "I believe 'e met your wife."

43

➤ He's so empty-headed there's nothing between his ears except his hearing aid.

➤ An advertising firm lost the account of a hearing aid manufacturer when it was learned they were advertising the product on the radio!

"Do You Hear Me?"

THE BORN LOSER ®by Art Sansom

BORN LOSER reprinted by permission of Newspaper Enterprise Association, Inc.

A Little Story

 A young reporter was assigned to do a story about boot camp training. At the nearby army camp, he watched a drill sergeant training a rookie squad to march.

"Sound off!" the sergeant commanded, and the squad responded. "Louder!" he yelled, in the best tradition of drillmasters getting all the enthusiasm possible from rookies, and the men raised the volume of their cadence. "LOUDER!" the sergeant shouted, "I still can't hear you!" The men doubled the sound of their count-off, and the sergeant roared back his approval, "That's better! *Now* I can hear you!"

After the sergeant dismissed the squad, the reporter came over to him and said, "Excuse me sir, but, uh... have you ever considered wearing a hearing aid?"

➤ This ad was seen recently in a newspaper personal section: "Pretty, smart, HOH WF seeks 30ish WM for love and companionship, possible marriage. Ex drill sergeants given special attention."

➤ Some products should have a warning label on them for the person who is HOH. I once got an ear infection trying to get close enough to hear the "snap, crackle, and pop" in a bowl of Rice Krispies.

INTERMISSION:

Now that you find humor can exist in what might otherwise be frustrating experiences, be aware that there are many, many other persons in the same boat as you. Though you may feel you're traveling stearage class because of your disability, be comforted by the fact that you're surrounded by others with the same problems who are both sympathetic and understanding.

Such awareness can improve both your outlook and the quality of your life. That is very important, for here's something to remember:

Laugh aloud, and the world laughs with you.

*Cry aloud, and suddenly **everyone** is hard of hearing.*

Ad-Venture:

From a classified advertisement in the Ventnor, NJ, *Post:* "*Attention antique dealers*—elderly gentleman, disillusioned with modern hearing aids, seeks old-fashioned ear trumpet. Call 555-9361, and *SPEAK UP!*"

"I said, 'Is that the three hundred dollar hearing aid you sent for?'"

51

➤ It's better to misplace a hearing aid than a pair of glasses. You don't have to be wearing the hearing aid in order to find it.

➤ Can you believe it? A judge tried a hearing aid—and found it guilty!

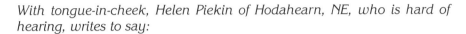

With tongue-in-cheek, Helen Piekin of Hodahearn, NE, who is hard of hearing, writes to say:

I prefer to think of myself as "easy of misunderstanding" rather than "hard of hearing." Sometimes I envy the deaf; they at least have their own subculture or society, while I live in a twilight zone, neither "hear" nor there. I believe it would be appropriate to say I feel "excommunicated" from the world in general.

And it pleases me to boast that mine is a "multilingual hearing disability," since I don't hear Spanish just as well as I don't hear Italian or French, but I don't hear Russian best of all!

A Little Story

➤ A spinster librarian visited her old family doctor one day. He asked her what her problem was and she said, "It's so embarrassing I don't know how to explain it to you."

"Come now," the doctor said. "You've been my patient for so long, certainly you should be able to tell me all about it."

"I know," she said, "but it's something I really can't bring myself to talk about."

"Edith," the doctor replied, "I brought you into this world. I've treated you and your whole family for all these many years; what can it be that's bothering you so greatly?"

Gathering herself together and with her eyes averted, she said, "I have gas."

"Edith," the doctor said, "everyone has gas."

"I know," she replied, "but I have an awful lot of gas."

"Many people have a lot of gas," the doctor assured her.

"I know," she said, "but I have so much that I'm constantly passing it. I have no control over it and it's even happening right now. Whatever shall I do about it? I'm afraid of offending people; thank goodness I'm at least able to keep it silent."

"Well Edith," the doctor said gently, "we'll take care of the gas, but the very, very first thing you must do is get yourself a good hearing aid."

M. Levison, Pittsburgh, PA, writes to say:

I have a recurring nightmare that scares the wits out of me, and it usually occurs on the night of a day during which I have bemoaned my bad hearing. Suddenly, miraculously, my hearing is restored and I am forced to listen to *everything* that goes on in this world. AAARRRRGH ! ! !

*"I don't believe you're hard of hearing. I **never** believed it!"*

A Little Story

➤ A flight attendant on a plane bound for Cincinnati found a passenger sitting in first class whose ticket called for coach seating. Twice she asked him to return to his proper seat, and twice he pointed to his ears and shook his head as though to indicate he was HOH and couldn't understand her.

The flight attendant went to the captain and explained the situation, saying, "I think he's just pretending to be hard of hearing, and simply trying to stay in first class."

The captain nodded, went back to the passenger, leaned over, and whispered something in his ear. The passenger immediately got up and returned to his seat in the coach section.

The flight attendant was curious and asked the captain just what he had said to the man.

"Not much," the captain replied. "All I said was, first class does not stop in Cincinnati."

A. Forman, Florida

The Trouble with Listening

When God gave out *brains,* I thought he said *trains*, and I missed mine.

When God gave out *looks*, I thought he said *books*, and I didn't want any.

When God gave out *noses*, I thought he said *roses*, and I asked for a red one.

When God gave out *legs*, I thought he said *kegs*, and I asked for two fat ones.

When God gave out *ears*, I thought he said *beers*, and I asked for two long ones.

When God gave out *chins*, I thought he said *gins*, and I ordered a double.

When God gave out *heads*, I thought he said *beds*, and I asked for a soft one.

...Since then, dear God, I will try to listen better.

Reprint from Cystic Fibrosis Flash, *March 1980*

➤ A man sitting next to his friend who is HOH says, "Can you lend me $250?" His friend replies, "I can't hear you, try my other ear." The man moves over to the other side, thinks a moment, shrugs, and says, "I said, can you lend me $500?" His friend turns to him, raises an eyebrow and pointedly says, "Go back to the first ear."

➤ Husband: "That cute blonde said I have the hearing of a police dog."

Wife: "Not really. She said you have the *ears* of a police dog."

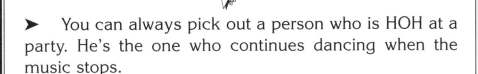

➤ You can always pick out a person who is HOH at a party. He's the one who continues dancing when the music stops.

➤ I know a man who is HOH who has the grip of a trapeze artist. Naturally, he hangs on to your every word!

➤ Another man who was HOH, wanting to overhear his neighbors, quietly climbed up on their roof. He got too close to the edge and fell off, and that's how the term *eavesdropping* originated.

➤ A police car with its lights flashing and siren wailing pulls up behind a man who is hard of hearing, who is driving too fast. The man doesn't see the lights flashing because his car is loaded with suitcases and clothes for his trip. The officer finally pulls him over by driving alongside and motioning to him.

"Didn't you see my lights?" the officer sternly asks.

"I'm sorry, there's so much stuff in back, I couldn't see."

"Then how about my siren? You didn't hear my siren?"

"No, I'm hard of hearing."

"Well, maybe you ought to get a hearing aid if you're going to drive so fast."

"Naah," the man replied. "Tickets are cheaper."

A. Forman, Florida

➤ For the person who is HOH, many sounds that were a part of daily life have faded away. To keep them from being permanently forgotten, try to recall the following sounds:

- the *call* of the wild
- an *explosion* of autumn colors
- Long Island *Sound*
- a financial *crunch*
- the *crack* of dawn
- a *blow* to your pride
- a heart*break*

"'When you deposited the 50 cents, did you hear a "clink" as it fell into our bucket? If not, you should seek professional help. Thank you.'"

67

➤ A young man who was HOH accidentally fell over the balcony of his 47th story apartment. As he passed the 23rd floor, an English gentleman called out to him and said, "I say old chap, why all the hurry?" The young man yelled back at him, "What did you SAAAAAY?"

A Little Story

➤ A man who was HOH took his attractive young wife to the doctor. She was complaining about chest pains. The doctor told the husband to wait in the reception room while his wife was examined.

Sometime later, the doctor called the husband into his private office, sat him down, and said, "I must tell you, your wife has acute angina."

The husband jumped up, furious, and said, "I ought to punch you in the nose! We told you the pains were in her *chest!*"

This note is from C. Slaw, Doylestown, PA:

I have found that in my dreams I seem to have perfectly normal hearing. Now my wife wonders why I spend so much time napping!

➤ Sigmund Freud, famous psychiatrist, had an operation that left him deaf in one ear. As a result, he turned his couch around so that his patients faced his good ear.

A colleague met him a few months later and said to him, "Well, Ziggy, so how are you getting along? Are you able to hear your patients?"

Freud looked up at him, smiled, and said, "Who listens?"

A Little Story

➤ A man goes into a bar with a beautiful Brazilian parrot on his shoulder. He sits down and the bartender asks if he can serve him. The guy says, "What?" The bartender asks the man again what he would like, and again the man says, "What? WHAT??"

The bartender shakes his head and starts to walk away. Suddenly the parrot says, "Sorry, Mac. Reggie doesn't hear too well. Give him a gin and tonic." The bartender, impressed, gets the drink.

As Reggie slurps the drink, the beautiful parrot talks about his former home in the jungle and how tough the flight up to the states had been. The bartender is fascinated by the parrot and without being asked, brings the man another drink.

The parrot goes on and on, bemoaning the loss of the Brazilian rain forest at great length while the bartender brings the man yet a third drink. The man finishes the drink and gets up to leave, and the bartender says, "That'll be fifteen bucks."

The parrot turns his head sideways to the bartender and shrieks, "Whadja say? What? WHAT??"

➤ One evening, a man who is HOH and his wife are watching television. She turns to him and says something that surprises him; they've been married 45 years and it's been a long time since she's made such a request. He gets up, walks over to her, and gives her a big kiss. Now it's her turn to be surprised.

"What was that for?" she asks. He says, "Didn't you say, "I want to kiss you?" "No, NO!" she replies. "I said I wanted a *tissue!*"

A. Forman, Florida

"Do You Hear Me?"

"So you saved seventeen bucks...still, wouldn't a regular hearing aid have been simpler?"

More Excerpts from the
"Do You Hear Me?" Dictione*ary*

Webster's	Our Spelling	Our *Deaf*inition
irritate	*ear*ritate	To overhear something unpleasant.
irrigate	*ear*rigate	To wash your ears.
irrelevant	*ear*relevant	Nothing to do with ears.

*Deaf*initions—Continued

Webster's	Our Spelling	Our *Deaf*inition
irretrievable	*ear*retrievable	Said and over with.
irrational	*ear*rational	What you hear makes no sense.
irresistible	*ear*resistible	Hear it and love it!

➤ A man who is HOH tells an acquaintance he's been married to the same woman for 55 years. The acquaintance asks if he has to put up with a lot of nagging. The HOH man says, "What?"

More Sounds the Hard of Hearing May Have Forgotten

- a *clash* of wills
- a *smashing* outfit
- the *bark* of trees
- money *talking*
- ginger*snaps*
- the *drip* you dated
- *shooting* stars
- a *dropped* hint

A Little Story

➤ A recent federal government report was critical of the driving skills of people who are HOH. The report stated that folks who are HOH tended to get confused easily, which caused them to lose their sense of direction. As a result, they often ended up hopelessly lost.

The folks who were HOH took the report as unfounded criticism. In New York City, they appointed a committee to drive to Washington to protest the conclusions of the report in front of the federal agency that had issued it.

When last heard from, the group of protesters was halfway to Seattle...Washington!

➤ Two opposing politicians were campaigning at the same time in the area in which I live. It so happened that the race was so close that mine was considered to be the crucial vote.

Both of them showed up at my house at the same time. When they realized I was HOH, both of them appealed to me by using megaphones. That was when I learned what it meant to "take the bull by the horns."

➤ Comedian Jackie Mason used to explain his large family like this:

"My parents used to live next to the railroad tracks, and my mother was HOH. Every morning at six, a freight train would come rumbling through, loud enough to wake them both up.

My father would turn to my mother and say, 'Do you want to go back to sleep, or what?'

To which my mother would reply, 'What?'"

"Do You Hear Me?"

"Now for heaven's sake, don't make an issue of his being hard of hearing!"

A Little Story

➤ A couple, who were HOH, retired to a farm from life in the city. They invited some of their city friends to spend a weekend with them.

The city friends were given a tour of the farm. They asked to see a demonstration of milking a cow. Then they wanted to see the pigs being fed. Next they had a walk through the barn and jumped into haystacks. This went on and on until it was time for dinner.

After they had eaten, there was a long night of conversation. Finally, the hostess said, "Well everyone, it's time to go to bed. I hope you won't be bored tomorrow now that you know everything there is to know about living on a farm."

"Oh, but we don't know everything there is to know about living on a farm, at least not yet," said one guest.

"What do you mean?" asked the hostess.

"We haven't been awakened by the crowing of the rooster. That will be the final touch," said the guest.

"Oh," the hostess replied. "I'm sorry. Our rooster gave up long ago trying to wake us by crowing; don't be surprised when he comes around at dawn and pecks you on the ear."

INTERMISSION:

Why is it that just about everyone who needs glasses wears them, while those with hearing problems tend to put off the wearing of hearing aids? Why the stigma? The reason is clear and simple: Hearing loss is associated with growing old, and we are reluctant to yield to aging. In addition, it's so very human to try to hide any disability, no matter what it is.

Glasses are so accepted that they are hardly noticed and have actually become designer items.

But it wasn't always that way. Just a few generations ago, there was resistance to them also. I can still remember when school kids wearing glasses were taunted, "Hey, four eyes!"

The day is fast coming when hearing aids will be as natural and accepted as glasses are now. Please, believe me:

An unassisted hearing problem is more noticeable than the hearing aid that could have helped it.

A Little Story

 I was in the kitchen one day, reading a newspaper and trying to carry on a conversation with my wife at the same time. Impossible! She'd say something and I'd ask her to repeat it; when she did, I'd reply, hoping it was the right answer and that if it weren't, she'd be a sport about it and forgive me. And so it went.

At one point there was a long lull, and then she spoke up again. I didn't understand her but I mumbled something to appease her, just enough to allow me to continue reading the paper. This went on for a bit until she distinctly changed her tone. This time I figured it was important enough to warrant putting down the paper. I looked up in order to read her lips and was shocked!

She wasn't in the kitchen!!

She had left the room after turning on the dishwasher, and I had been carrying on a conversation with the damned machine as it changed cycles. It was producing pretty much the same sounds my wife had been making!

Reggie Stambaugh, United Kingdom

➤ A New Year's resolution is something that goes in one y*ear* and out the other.

➤ Sign not yet seen in the window of a hearing aid shop, but appropriate enough: "Here today, hear tomorrow."

SURPRISE GIFT!

Free Hearing Aid and Instructions
Before making, read reverse side!

• • • •

You've read it and still wish to proceed?

1. Cut out page at heavy dotted line and then cut away other dotted lines.

2. Carefully roll into cone shape with small opening at one end and large opening at other. Secure with tape.

3. Place small end in ear, point large end toward the speaker. Listen carefully! Then decide if you really care to hear more. (Try not to allow your face to give your decision away!)

91

Surgeon General's Warning!

Listening with the hearing aid on the previous page can be hazardous to your health! The material employed is *not* fireproof!

Therefore, you are strongly advised to avoid *heated* arguments and *inflammatory* remarks!!!

"Do You Hear Me?"

BORN LOSER® by Art and Chip Sansom

➤ In letter writing, the time-honored phrase, "Looking forward to hearing from you in the near future," could properly be changed by the HOH to read, "Looking forward to *reading* you in the near future."

➤ Many an investor who is HOH has missed a *sound* investment!

➤ To keep me from brooding about my hearing loss, a friend gave me a dog who is also HOH so we could share our problem together. I had him fitted with a hearing aid, and I spend a good deal of my time seeing to it that he understands what's going on. The only problem is, I have to try to figure out when his battery needs replacement. Believe it or not, when I do replace his battery, his eyes light up!

Byron Gamble, Pennsylvania

A Little Story About Ears

 There was a great corn shortage in ancient Rome. It was at that time that Mark Antony gave his famous speech that began, "Friends, Romans, countrymen, lend me your ears."

This speech was quite effective and brought in a lot of corn, but it was not enough to meet the demand. As a result, it was necessary to resort to rationing. An edict went out whereby each person could eat only one ear a week.

Because he was the head man, Caesar did not think the rationing rules applied to him, and one day he ate more than his ration.

Upon hearing this, Brutus called on Caesar and said, "Caesar, how much corn did you eat?" That was the historic occasion when Caesar replied, "Et two, Brutus."

A Little Story

 A lumberjack is in the forest, chopping down a huge old tree: "Chop-chop-chop, chop-chop-chop." Then he steps back and shouts, "Timber!" Nothing happens.

Once again, "Chop-chop-chop, chop-chop-chop," and once again he shouts, *"Timber!"* Again, nothing happens.

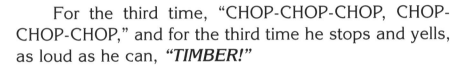

For the third time, "CHOP-CHOP-CHOP, CHOP-CHOP-CHOP," and for the third time he stops and yells, as loud as he can, *"TIMBER!"*

Still, nothing happens. He gets a sudden inspiration. Stepping back even further, he raises his right hand toward the tree and slowly finger spells T-I-M-B-E-R. The ancient tree trembles, shudders, and comes crashing down.

➤ Everyone knows how frustrating it can be to have a word dangling "on the tip of one's tongue." Much the same thing occurs when the HOH have asked two or three times, for a word that still eludes them, to be repeated. Couldn't the term for that predicament be, "It's on the lobe of my ear"?

➤ A woman, who was HOH, and her husband were listening to a radio news broadcast, and the woman turned to her husband in alarm. "Where did the attacks on pleasure boats take place?" she asked him. "They didn't say *attacks,*" he replied. "They said they're considering a *tax* on pleasure boats."

➤ There is now a hearing aid with a built-in echo. It's great for hearing things the second or third time.

➤ A man who was HOH had to give up drinking. He was into the icemaker so often that his hearing aid malfunctioned when the circuits froze.

➤ An HOH woman explains why she's not much of a shopper: "That's because in the little town I come from, all the advertising is by word of mouth."

➤ If it's true that money talks, will somebody *please* tell me what it's saying?

A Little Story

➤ A man comes into his regular bar, greets the bartender, places a box on the counter, and asks for a double martini. As he sips the drink, he sighs and shakes his head.

The bartender looks at him and asks him if it's what's in the box that is bothering him.

The man looks up at the bartender, nods, and says, "I'm going to show you something you won't believe."

Opening the carton, he takes out a miniature grand piano, complete with stool, and sets it on the counter. Then he reaches in again and brings out a tiny man, no more than a foot tall, and places him at the piano. Immediately, the little man starts playing a selection on the piano.

The bartender is astounded. "Where in the world did you ever get such a thing?" he asks.

The customer says, "I was walking in the park and I met a leprechaun. We struck up a conversation. The leprechaun told me he liked me and that he would grant me one wish if I told him what my heart's desire was."

Slowly shaking his head, the man continued. "He must have been hard of hearing. I guess he thought I asked for a 12-inch pianist."

A. Forman, Florida

➤ There's a good reason why I've never made much of my life: Every time opportunity knocked, I was in the shower with my hearing aid on the sink.

➤ A friend of mine asked me if I liked battery watches better than the old ones that ticked. *Watches ticked?*

"Do You Hear Me?"

BORN LOSER® by Art and Chip Sansom

A Little Story

➤ A man who was HOH was told by his doctor to stop drinking brandy. According to the doctor, the brandy was making his hearing worse.

For a pretty good while, the man followed the doctor's instructions, but after a few months he went back to drinking.

When his doctor demanded to know why, he said, "You were right. As long as I didn't drink, I was able to hear better, but nothing I heard was as good as the brandy."

More Sounds the Hard of Hearing May Have Forgotten

- a *burst* of energy
- a *big shot*
- orange and lemon "*peals*"
- eyes *popping*
- the *blast* the party was
- ice *scream*
- a wise*crack*
- a *ring* around the bathtub

A Little Story

➤ When Tom Harte, a Utah Republican, was running for a third term in Congress, he spotted a farmer leaning on a fence post and stopped to shake hands and introduce himself.

"I'm Tom Harte, your congressman," he said.

The farmer, who was quite HOH, said, "You're who?"

Smith replied, "I'm your congressman, Tom Harte."

The farmer still looked puzzled. Trying a new tack, Harte bellowed, "I'm running for Congress and I'd like to have your vote!"

The old farmer's face brightened and he said, "I don't know who you are son, but I'll be glad to vote for you. The feller we've got in there now isn't worth a damn!"

A Little Story

 A mother and her eight-year-old daughter who is HOH hail a cab in San Francisco. The mother and daughter sit up front with the driver, who notices the child's hearing aid.

He strikes up a conversation about the problems of living with a disability.

They are rocketing down one of the steepest hills in Frisco when he turns to the girl and says, "Don't let being hard of hearing keep you from doing whatever you want. I lead a normal life, and I'm almost blind."

Shirley Albright, California

"There's Thor. Pretend you don't notice his hearing aids."

113

A Little Story

➤ My father, who is HOH, underwent an operation. A day or two later when I went to visit him, I waited quietly outside the door while his nurse finished bathing him. It was obvious she enjoyed him as a person, for I overheard her say soothingly to him, "I wish I had a thousand patients like you."

"What did you say?" my father asked.

The nurse paused, raised her voice, and said, "I wish I had a hundred patients like you."

"I'm sorry," said father, "I still didn't hear you."

The nurse, still louder, but this time with an edge to her voice, replied, "I said, I wish I had another patient like you."

Sander Lazar, Salt Lake City, UT

Lea Lawrence of Ranklin, TN, has this to say:

When I order food in a noisy restaurant, I try to cover everything without the waiter asking additional questions, since that will confuse the issue. But they always come back with some question or other that I can't hear, and I usually end up frustratedly saying, "Yes." Now, *that* can be *dangerous!* Let me tell you why.

Here are just a few of the things saying yes can bring about:

- a $95 bottle of wine
- French-fried zucchini in cherry sauce
- a Gypsy violinist
- a mini-skirted photographer
- etc., etc.

A Little Story

➤ Jack was an avid runner. He was a little HOH but was reluctant to wear a hearing aid. As a result, it was necessary to talk in a loud voice whenever speaking to him.

In April, Jack was due to fly with other members of his running club to compete in the famed Boston Marathon.

The club trainer had promised to bring a particular muscle liniment called Miracle Balm that Jack found to be very effective. When Jack saw the trainer at the airport he called out to him, "Did you bring the balm?"

Remembering that Jack was HOH, the trainer responded in a loud voice, *"Yes, I put the balm in my luggage."*

At that point, the security guards descended on Jack and the trainer...

More Excerpts from the
"Do You Hear Me?" Diction*ear*y

Webster's	Our Spelling	Our *Dea*finition
ambidextrous	ambidext*ear*ous	The ability to hear just as poorly with either ear.
conference	conf*ear*ence	An opportunity not to hear many people simultaneously.

*Deaf*initions—Continued

Webster's	Our Spelling	Our *Deaf*inition
aerobics	*ear*obics	Exercising to music you can't hear.
cheerful	ch*ear*ful	Good news, easily heard.
eternity	et*ear*nity	The time that passes as the HOH try to answer a question they didn't hear.

A Little Story

➤ A heavyset woman was in a sporting goods store looking for a gift for her boyfriend. All she had was $40 and she was having a hard time finding something for that price.

She liked a certain fishing rod that cost $38, but the reel for it cost $50. She stood for a moment, looking around. Seeing no one near, she stuffed the reel into her bra and headed for the checkout counter.

As the cashier reached for the rod, it slipped on the counter and fell at the woman's feet. The woman bent over to pick it up, and the reel fell out and landed on the floor. At the same time, the exertion caused her to expel a noisy gust of gas.

The cashier looked at her sternly and said, "I want you to know I'm *not* hard of hearing. That'll be $38 for the rod, $50 for the reel, and $5.95 for the *duck* call, *wherever* you've got it hidden!"

➤ During the physical examination of a young girl who was HOH, the doctor places his stethoscope on her chest and says, "Deep breaths."

"Yes," she says as she smiles proudly, "and I'm only thirteen."

➤ If you're going to try to play the piano by ear, be sure to remove your hearing aid first. (Think about it!)

F. Savoy from Ontario, Canada writes to say:

➤   I'm never too long on the telephone. I'm usually able to misunderstand everything that's to be said in the first minute or two of conversation.

• • • • • • •

1st Man: "Last night I talked in my sleep."
2nd Man: "What'd you say?"
1st Man: "I don't know. I wasn't wearing my
             hearing aid."

➤ A fellow who is HOH says he's confused by the old proverb of the "three monkeys." He says he is willing to "speak no evil" and to "see no evil," but he says he cannot "hear no evil"!

"No, what I said was, 'I'm feeling rheumatic'!"

➤ The hard of hearing would like to see the country observe a "National Hearing Impaired Week," during which the national anthem would be temporarily changed to, "Ohhh say can you hear...?"

And That's It, Folks!

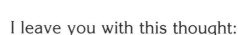

I leave you with this thought:

Each and every one of us has a problem of one sort or another. It is how we cope with that problem that determines both our outlook and the quality of our lives.

Notes about the Author/Editor

Maxwell Schneider, a past president of the Consumers Organization for the Hearing Impaired (COHI), has devoted much of his time to the interests of the hard of hearing. He is intimately familiar with the problems of what is properly called "the invisible handicap." Here's what he has to say about his book:

Because there really is nothing amusing about being hearing impaired, it became more and more important that this book become a reality and not just left as an idea that had floated around in my head for so many years. I felt certain that the HOH would relate to the situations depicted in the book, and the realization that so many others share the same problems with them would then serve to reduce their tensions and frustrations. Once the book serves that purpose, it will still have achieved only a portion of my real goal.

It is a well-known fact that individuals with an existing or developing hearing impairment often are reluctant to admit the problem exists, and that when they finally do, they are hesitant about turning to all the wonderful professional help and marvelous devices available to them.

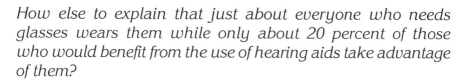

How else to explain that just about everyone who needs glasses wears them while only about 20 percent of those who would benefit from the use of hearing aids take advantage of them?

It is also a fact that when failing hearing remains unattended, the usual sad result is an individual who drifts farther and farther out of the "mainstream." Additionally, the longer the problem is ignored, the more difficult it is to help.

Moreover, and most unfortunately, it isn't only the individual who is being done a disservice. To the figure of 24 million who are HOH must be added all those millions of friends and family members who also tend to become more and more burdened.

*Therefore, my second and most overriding goal is to urge the individual to **do something about it!** And it must be borne in mind that family members and friends offering sympathetic and understanding encouragement can play an extremely important role in the decision to seek the necessary professional help.*

For assistance, individuals who are HOH or their friends or family members can write to or call the following organizations:

ALEXANDER GRAHAM BELL ASSOCIATION
3417 Volta Place, N.W.
Washington, DC 20007-2778
1-202-337-5220 (Voice or TTY)
www.agbell.org

AMERICAN SPEECH-LANGUAGE-HEARING ASSOCIATION
10801 Rockville Pike
Rockville, MD 20852
1-800-638-8255 (Voice or TTY)
www.asha.org

AMERICAN ACADEMY OF AUDIOLOGY
8201 Greensboro Drive, Suite 300
McLean, VA 22102
1-800-222-2336
www.audiology.com

AMERICAN ACADEMY OF OTOLARYNGOLOGY
One Prince Street
Alexandria, VA 22314-3357
1-703-836-4444 or 1-703-519-1585 (TTY)
www.entnet.org

AMERICAN TINNITUS ASSOCIATION
1618 SW 1st Avenue #417
Portland, OR 97201
1-503-248-9985
www.teleport.com\~ata

BETTER HEARING INSTITUTE
5021-B Backlick Road
Annandale, VA 22003
1-800-EAR-WELL (Hearing Helpline; Voice or TTY)
Hearing Help-On-Line www.betterhearing.org

HEAR NOW
9745 E. Hampden Ave. #300
Denver, CO 80231-4923
1-800-648-HEAR or 1-303-695-7797 (Voice or TTY)
www.leisurelan.com/~hearnow/

INTERNATIONAL HEARING SOCIETY
20361 Middlebelt Road
Livonia, MI 48152
1-800-521-5247 (Hearing Aid Helpline)

SELF HELP FOR HARD OF HEARING PEOPLE
7910 Woodmont Ave., Suite 1200
Bethesda, MD 20814
1-301-657-2248 (Voice) or 1-301-657-2249 (TTY)
www.shhh.org

If you have HOH humor similar to the type found in *"Do You Hear Me?"*, I will be happy to consider it for the next edition. Please send submissions to

> Thinking Publications
> Attn: Maxwell Schneider
> P.O. Box 163
> Eau Claire, WI 54702-0163
>
> E-mail: editors@ThinkingPublications.com